Words To Live By

100 Inspirational Quotes That Illuminate the Human Experience, Spark Change, and Empower the Soul"

Mo.Gad

"Words are, of course, the most powerful drug used by mankind."

— Rudyard Kipling

Introduction :

Words have the power to heal, inspire, and ignite change. Throughout history, great thinkers, writers, and leaders have captured the essence of human experience in just a few sentences. In this collection, you will find a blend of wisdom, humor, and profound insights that span cultures and eras. These quotes are more than just words; they are sparks of light that illuminate our journey through life. May this book serve as a source of encouragement, comfort, and motivation as you navigate your own path.

1-"Life is 10% what happens to us and 90% how we react to it."

— Charles R. Swindoll

Comment:

This quote emphasizes the power of perspective. While we can't control every event, we do have the power to shape our responses, which ultimately determines our experiences. It serves as a reminder to focus on our mindset and how we handle life's challenges.

Overview of the Person:

Charles R. Swindoll is an American pastor, author, and educator known for his practical and encouraging messages. His teachings often focus on the importance of attitude and personal growth.

2-*"You can't go back and change the beginning, but you can start where you are and change the ending."*

— *C.S. Lewis*

Comment:

This quote reflects the power of choice in shaping our future. It encourages us to take action despite past mistakes or setbacks, focusing instead on what we can control moving forward. It's a powerful message about embracing personal agency and creating a new path.

Overview of the Person:

C.S. Lewis was a British writer and scholar best known for his works on Christian apologetics and the classic series *The Chronicles of Narnia*. His writings often explore themes of faith, morality, and the human condition.

3-"Be yourself; everyone else is already taken."

— Oscar Wilde

Comment:

This quote is a witty reminder to embrace authenticity. It encourages us to appreciate our unique qualities rather than conforming to others' expectations. Being true to oneself is not only more fulfilling but also allows for genuine connections with others.

Overview of the Person:

Oscar Wilde was an Irish poet, playwright, and novelist known for his sharp wit and flamboyant style. His works often challenged social norms and celebrated individuality.

4-"Success is not the key to happiness. Happiness is the key to success. If you love what you are doing, you will be successful."

— Albert Schweitzer

Comment:

This quote flips the common narrative, suggesting that happiness fuels success rather than the other way around. Finding joy in one's work or passion can lead to fulfillment, which is often reflected in outward achievements.

Overview of the Person:

Albert Schweitzer was a German theologian, physician, and Nobel Peace Prize laureate. He dedicated much of his life to humanitarian work, particularly in medical missions, and is remembered for his philosophy of "reverence for life."

5- "Don't watch the clock; do what it does. Keep going."

— Sam Levenson

Comment:

This quote serves as a reminder to stay focused on progress rather than the passage of time. It encourages perseverance and consistent effort, qualities that lead to long-term success.

Overview of the Person:

Sam Levenson was an American humorist, writer, and television host. His comedic style often included practical wisdom, making his observations both entertaining and insightful.

6-"If you think you are too small to make a difference, try sleeping with a mosquito."

— *Dalai Lama*

Comment:

Even the smallest actions can have a significant impact. This humorous yet profound saying encourages individuals to recognize their potential for creating change, regardless of their size or status.

Overview of the Person:

The Dalai Lama is the spiritual leader of Tibetan Buddhism and a prominent advocate for peace and human rights. His teachings emphasize compassion, mindfulness, and the power of small acts.

7-"The purpose of life is not to be happy. It is to be useful, to be honorable, to be compassionate, to have it make some difference that you have lived and lived well."

— *Ralph Waldo Emerson*

Comment:

This quote shifts the focus from personal happiness to living a life of purpose. It encourages striving for a meaningful existence through service, integrity, and empathy, which ultimately leads to a fulfilling life.

Overview of the Person:

Ralph Waldo Emerson was an American essayist, philosopher, and poet who led the transcendentalist movement. His works explore themes of individualism, nature, and spirituality.

8-"If opportunity doesn't knock, build a door."

— Milton Berle

Comment:

Rather than waiting for chances to come your way, this quote encourages proactive behavior. It inspires creativity and initiative, reminding us that we can create opportunities through effort and ingenuity.

Overview of the Person:

Milton Berle was a legendary American comedian and actor, known for his quick wit and role in the early days of television. His humor often contained kernels of wisdom, reflecting his approach to life.

9-*"The best way to predict the future is to create it."*

— Peter Drucker

Comment:

This quote emphasizes the importance of taking initiative in shaping one's destiny. Rather than waiting for circumstances to change, we have the power to influence our future through our actions and decisions. It serves as a call to be proactive and intentional in pursuing our goals.

Overview of the Person:

Peter Drucker was an influential management consultant, educator, and author, known for his writings on management theory and practice. He is often referred to as the father of modern management.

10-"What lies behind us and what lies before us are tiny matters compared to what lies within us."

— Ralph Waldo Emerson

Comment:

This quote highlights the significance of inner strength and character over external circumstances. It encourages self-reflection and the acknowledgment of our inner resources, suggesting that true power comes from within, regardless of past or future challenges.

Overview of the Person:

Ralph Waldo Emerson was an American essayist, philosopher, and poet who led the transcendentalist movement. His works explore themes of individualism, nature, and spirituality.

11-"Success usually comes to those who are too busy to be looking for it."

— Henry David Thoreau

Comment:

This quote suggests that success often results from hard work and dedication rather than a singular focus on achieving it. It encourages us to immerse ourselves in our passions and pursuits, allowing success to follow naturally.

Overview of the Person:

Henry David Thoreau was an American essayist, poet, and philosopher known for his book *Walden*, which reflects his transcendentalist beliefs and his advocacy for simple living in natural surroundings.

12-"To live is the rarest thing in the world. Most people exist, that is all."

— *Oscar Wilde*

Comment:

Wilde's observation highlights the difference between merely surviving and truly living. It encourages us to seek a deeper, more fulfilling existence rather than simply going through the motions, reminding us of the importance of authenticity.

Overview of the Person:

Oscar Wilde was an Irish poet, playwright, and novelist known for his sharp wit and flamboyant style. His works often challenged social norms and celebrated individuality.

13-"Out of chaos comes order."

— Friedrich Nietzsche

Comment:

This quote speaks to the transformative power of chaos in life. It suggests that through struggle and disorder, we can find new perspectives and create meaning. Embracing chaos can lead to growth and change.

Overview of the Person:

Friedrich Nietzsche was a German philosopher known for his provocative ideas about morality, culture, and existentialism. His writings often explore themes of individuality and the human condition.

14-"We are all in the gutter, but some of us are looking at the stars."

— Oscar Wilde

Comment:

This quote reflects the duality of human experience, acknowledging that while we may face difficulties, maintaining hope and aspiration can lift us above our circumstances. It encourages us to seek beauty and inspiration even in dark times.

Overview of the Person:

Oscar Wilde was an Irish poet, playwright, and novelist known for his sharp wit and flamboyant style. His works often challenged social norms and celebrated individuality.

15-"The wound is the place where the Light enters you."

— Rumi

Comment:

Rumi's quote emphasizes that our pain and suffering can lead to growth and enlightenment. It suggests that through our struggles, we can find wisdom and healing, encouraging a perspective shift on adversity.

Overview of the Person:

Rumi was a 13th-century Persian poet and Sufi mystic, known for his profound spiritual insights and lyrical poetry that continues to resonate across cultures and ages.

16-*"We are what we repeatedly do. Excellence, then, is not an act, but a habit."*

— Aristotle

Comment:

This quote emphasizes the importance of consistency in our actions. It suggests that achieving greatness is not a one-time event but rather a culmination of our daily habits and choices.

Overview of the Person:

Aristotle was an ancient Greek philosopher and polymath whose teachings have influenced Western thought for centuries. His works cover a wide range of topics, including ethics, politics, and metaphysics.

17-"In three words, I can sum up everything I've learned about life: it goes on."

— *Robert Frost*

Frost's succinct observation captures the inevitability of life's progression. It serves as a reminder that despite challenges and hardships, life continues, encouraging us to embrace change and resilience.

Robert Frost was an American poet known for his depictions of rural New England life and his command of colloquial speech. His works often explore complex themes of nature and human emotion.

18-"It is only in our decisions that we are truly free."

— *Abraham Lincoln*

Comment:

Lincoln's quote emphasizes the power of choice in shaping our lives. It reminds us that freedom comes not just from external circumstances but from our ability to make decisions that reflect our values and aspirations.

Overview of the Person:

Abraham Lincoln was the 16th President of the United States, known for leading the country during the Civil War and for his efforts to abolish slavery. His leadership and vision for a united nation continue to inspire.

19-"Out of suffering have emerged the strongest souls; the most massive characters are seared with scars."

— *Khalil Gibran*

Comment:

Gibran's quote highlights the transformative power of suffering. It suggests that our struggles can shape our character and resilience, encouraging us to embrace our scars as symbols of strength.

Overview of the Person:

Khalil Gibran was a Lebanese-American poet, writer, and philosopher, best known for his book *The Prophet*. His writings explore themes of love, loss, and the human experience.

20-"You cannot find peace by avoiding life."

— *Virginia Woolf*

Comment:

Woolf's quote emphasizes the importance of engaging with life's challenges. It suggests that true peace comes from confronting our experiences rather than fleeing from them, encouraging us to embrace the complexity of existence.

Overview of the Person:

Virginia Woolf was an English writer and modernist known for her contributions to literature and feminist thought. Her works often explore the inner lives of women and the intricacies of human relationships.

21-"The mystery of human existence lies not in just staying alive, but in finding something to live for."

— *Fyodor Dostoevsky*

Comment:

Dostoevsky's quote emphasizes the search for purpose in life. It suggests that mere survival is insufficient; true fulfillment comes from pursuing passions and meaningful connections.

Overview of the Person:

Fyodor Dostoevsky was a Russian novelist and philosopher whose works delve into psychology and morality. His most famous novels include *Crime and Punishment* and *The Brothers Karamazov*.

22-"The more a man knows, the more he will realize he knows nothing."

— Arthur Schopenhauer

Comment:

Schopenhauer's quote reflects the paradox of knowledge. It suggests that true wisdom comes from recognizing the limits of our understanding, encouraging humility in the pursuit of knowledge.

Overview of the Person:

Arthur Schopenhauer was a German philosopher known for his pessimistic philosophy and the concept of the "will to live." His influential works include *The World as Will and Representation*.

23-*"The best way to find yourself is to lose yourself in the service of others."*

— *Mahatma Gandhi*

Comment:

Gandhi's quote emphasizes the transformative power of altruism. It suggests that true self-discovery often comes through serving and uplifting others, fostering a sense of connection and purpose.

Overview of the Person:

Mahatma Gandhi was an Indian leader known for his philosophy of nonviolent resistance. His efforts to achieve Indian independence from British rule have left a lasting legacy of peace and social justice.

24-*"If you want to know the character of a man, give him power."*

— Abraham Lincoln

Comment:

Lincoln's quote highlights the revealing nature of power. It suggests that true character is often exposed in positions of authority, encouraging vigilance in leadership and governance.

Overview of the Person:

Abraham Lincoln served as the 16th President of the United States and is renowned for his leadership during the Civil War and his commitment to abolishing slavery, leaving an indelible mark on American history.

25-*"What we achieve inwardly will change outer reality."*

— Plutarch

Comment:

Plutarch's quote emphasizes the transformative power of inner growth. It suggests that our internal state significantly influences our external circumstances, encouraging us to focus on personal development.

Overview of the Person:

Plutarch was a Greek biographer and philosopher known for his works on ethics and morality. His *Parallel Lives* compares the lives of famous Greeks and Romans, providing insights into character and virtue.

26-"To be yourself in a world that is constantly trying to make you something else is the greatest accomplishment."

— *Ralph Waldo Emerson*

Comment:

Emerson's quote speaks to the challenge of authenticity in a conformist society. It encourages us to embrace our individuality and resist external pressures to change.

Overview of the Person:

Ralph Waldo Emerson was a 19th-century American essayist and philosopher known for his advocacy of transcendentalism, emphasizing individuality and self-reliance.

27-*"Happiness is not something ready-made. It comes from your own actions."*

— Dalai Lama

Comment:

The Dalai Lama's quote emphasizes that happiness is a product of our choices and actions. It encourages us to take responsibility for our well-being and actively pursue joy.

Overview of the Person:

The Dalai Lama is the spiritual leader of Tibetan Buddhism and a global advocate for peace and compassion. His teachings emphasize kindness, mindfulness, and the pursuit of happiness.

28-"Success is not final, failure is not fatal: It is the courage to continue that counts."

— Winston S. Churchill

Comment:

Churchill's quote highlights the importance of perseverance. It reminds us that both success and failure are temporary, but the determination to keep going is what truly matters.

Overview of the Person:

Winston S. Churchill was a British statesman and Prime Minister known for his leadership during World War II. His speeches and writings continue to inspire resilience and courage.

29-"The greatest weapon against stress is our ability to choose one thought over another."

— William James

Comment:

James' quote underscores the power of choice in managing our mental well-being. It suggests that we can alleviate stress by consciously shifting our thoughts and perspectives.

Overview of the Person:

William James was an American philosopher and psychologist known for his work in pragmatism and functionalism. His writings, including *The Principles of Psychology*, laid the foundation for modern psychology.

30-"To be yourself is all that you can do."

— Audioslave (Chris Cornell)

Comment:

Cornell's quote encourages authenticity and self-acceptance. It serves as a reminder that the most valuable thing we can offer the world is our true selves.

Overview of the Person:

Chris Cornell was an American musician and singer-songwriter known for his powerful voice and as the frontman of bands like Soundgarden and Audioslave. His lyrics often explored themes of identity and emotion.

31-"The way to get started is to quit talking and begin doing."

— Walt Disney

Comment:

Disney's quote underscores the importance of action over mere discussion. It encourages us to take the first step toward our goals rather than procrastinating.

Overview of the Person:

Walt Disney was an American entrepreneur, animator, and film producer known for founding the Disney entertainment empire. His innovative work in animation and theme parks revolutionized the industry.

32-"Do not dwell in the past, do not dream of the future, concentrate the mind on the present moment."

— *Buddha*

Comment:

Buddha's quote advocates for mindfulness and living in the present. It encourages us to let go of regrets and anxieties, focusing instead on the here and now.

Overview of the Person:

Buddha, or Siddhartha Gautama, was a spiritual leader who founded Buddhism. His teachings focus on the path to enlightenment and the alleviation of suffering through mindfulness and compassion.

33-"I am not what happened to me. I am what I choose to become."

— Carl Jung

Comment:

Jung's quote emphasizes the power of choice and self-determination. It serves as a reminder that we are not defined by our past but by how we respond to it.

Overview of the Person:

Carl Jung was a Swiss psychiatrist and psychoanalyst who founded analytical psychology. His work on the unconscious, archetypes, and personality has had a profound influence on psychology and spirituality.

34-"It does not matter how slowly you go as long as you do not stop."

— Confucius

Comment:

Confucius' quote emphasizes persistence and resilience. It reminds us that progress, no matter how gradual, is still a step toward our goals.

Overview of the Person:

Confucius was a Chinese philosopher whose teachings focused on ethics, family, and social harmony. His ideas have deeply influenced East Asian culture and thought.

35-"You cannot swim for new horizons until you have courage to lose sight of the shore."

— *William Faulkner*

Comment:

Faulkner's quote encourages us to embrace change and take risks. It reminds us that pursuing new opportunities often requires letting go of our comfort zones.

Overview of the Person:

William Faulkner was an American writer known for his complex narratives and innovative writing style, particularly in works like *The Sound and the Fury* and *As I Lay Dying*.

36-"Everything you can imagine is real."

— Pablo Picasso

Comment:

Picasso's quote speaks to the power of imagination and creativity. It encourages us to explore our visions and transform our ideas into reality.

Overview of the Person:

Pablo Picasso was a Spanish painter, sculptor, and co-founder of the Cubist movement, whose innovative works have made him one of the most influential artists of the 20th century.

37-"Do not wait to strike till the iron is hot, but make it hot by striking."

— William Butler Yeats

Comment:

Yeats' quote emphasizes the importance of initiative and action. It encourages us to create our own opportunities through effort and determination.

Overview of the Person:

William Butler Yeats was an Irish poet and playwright who was a key figure in the Irish literary revival and won the Nobel Prize in Literature in 1923.

38-"Success is not the key to happiness. Happiness is the key to success."

— *Albert Schweitzer*

Comment:

Schweitzer's quote suggests that true fulfillment comes from happiness, which, in turn, fuels success. It encourages us to prioritize our well-being over external achievements.

Overview of the Person:

Albert Schweitzer was a German-French theologian, philosopher, and physician known for his humanitarian work and philosophy of "Reverence for Life." He received the Nobel Peace Prize in 1952.

39-"You must be the change you wish to see in the world."

— Mahatma Gandhi

Comment:

Gandhi's quote emphasizes personal responsibility in creating positive change. It serves as a reminder that our actions can inspire others and contribute to a better world.

Overview of the Person:

Mahatma Gandhi was an Indian leader known for his nonviolent resistance to British rule. His philosophy of peace and civil disobedience has inspired movements for civil rights globally.

40-*"Dream big and dare to fail."*

— Norman Vaughan

Comment:

Vaughan's quote encourages us to pursue ambitious dreams without fear of failure. It reminds us that taking risks is essential for achieving greatness.

Overview of the Person:

Norman Vaughan was an American explorer and adventurer known for his expeditions to Antarctica and his adventurous spirit, which inspired others to pursue their dreams.

41-*"The best way to predict your future is to create it."*

— Peter Drucker

Comment:

Drucker's quote underscores the importance of taking proactive steps to shape our destinies. It encourages us to take charge of our lives and actively work toward our goals.

Overview of the Person:

Peter Drucker was an Austrian-American management consultant, educator, and author, widely considered the father of modern management. His insights have transformed business practices.

42-*"The only real mistake is the one from which we learn nothing."*

— Henry Ford

Comment:

Ford's quote highlights the importance of learning from our experiences. It encourages us to view mistakes as opportunities for growth and improvement.

Overview of the Person:

Henry Ford was an American industrialist and founder of Ford Motor Company, known for revolutionizing the automobile industry through assembly line production and his focus on efficiency.

43-"The only impossible journey is the one you never begin."

— *Tony Robbins*

Comment:

Robbins' quote emphasizes the importance of starting our journeys. It encourages us to take the leap and pursue our dreams without being hindered by fear of failure.

Overview of the Person:

Tony Robbins is an American author, entrepreneur, and motivational speaker known for his self-help books and seminars focused on personal development and empowerment.

44-"If you want to lift yourself up, lift up someone else."

— *Booker T. Washington*

Comment:

Washington's quote emphasizes the interconnectedness of success and generosity. It reminds us that helping others can elevate our own lives.

Overview of the Person:

Booker T. Washington was an African American educator and leader who founded the Tuskegee Institute and advocated for vocational training and self-reliance.

45-"Everything has beauty, but not everyone sees it."

— Confucius

Comment:

This quote encourages mindfulness and appreciation of the world around us. It reminds us that beauty exists in many forms, often waiting to be discovered.

Overview of the Person:

Confucius' teachings emphasize the importance of observation and appreciation of life, encouraging us to seek deeper understanding and connection.

46-"Success is how high you bounce when you hit bottom."

— General George S. Patton

Comment:

Patton's quote emphasizes resilience in the face of adversity. It reminds us that our ability to recover from setbacks defines our true success.

Overview of the Person:

General George S. Patton was a prominent U.S. Army general known for his leadership during World War II and his outspoken and bold personality.

47-"What we fear doing most is usually what we most need to do."

— *Tim Ferriss*

Comment:

Ferriss' quote encourages us to confront our fears head-on. It suggests that tackling the things that scare us can lead to significant personal growth.

Overview of the Person:

Tim Ferriss is an American author and entrepreneur known for his book *The 4-Hour Workweek* and for exploring productivity and self-improvement strategies.

48-"I'm selfish, impatient and a little insecure. I make mistakes, I am out of control and at times hard to handle. But if you can't handle me at my worst, then you sure as hell don't deserve me at my best."

— Marilyn Monroe

Comment:

Monroe's quote emphasizes authenticity and the complexity of human nature. It serves as a reminder that everyone has flaws, and true acceptance requires embracing both the good and the bad.

Overview of the Person:

Marilyn Monroe was an American actress, model, and cultural icon known for her beauty, charisma, and significant impact on the film industry in the 1950s.

49-*"Two things are infinite: the universe and human stupidity; and I'm not sure about the universe."*

— Albert Einstein

Comment:

Einstein's quote humorously critiques human nature and highlights the vastness of ignorance. It serves as a reminder to approach life with a sense of curiosity and humility.

Overview of the Person:

Albert Einstein was a theoretical physicist renowned for developing the theory of relativity and for his profound influence on modern physics and philosophy.

50-*"Be who you are and say what you feel, because those who mind don't matter, and those who matter don't mind."*

— Bernard M. Baruch

Comment:

Baruch's quote encourages authenticity and self-expression. It reminds us that the opinions of those who truly care about us will not hinder our true selves.

Overview of the Person:

Bernard M. Baruch was an American financier, stock market speculator, and political consultant known for his influential role in the economic and political spheres during the 20th century.

51-"You've gotta dance like there's nobody watching,
Love like you'll never be hurt,
Sing like there's nobody listening,
And live like it's heaven on earth."

— William W. Purkey

Comment:

Purkey's quote encourages us to embrace life fully and authentically. It serves as a reminder to live with joy, passion, and fearlessness, without being constrained by the judgments of others.

Overview of the Person:

William W. Purkey is an American author and educator known for his work on positive psychology and self-acceptance, especially in educational settings.

52-"You know you're in love when you can't fall asleep because reality is finally better than your dreams."

— Dr. Seuss

Comment:

This quote by Dr. Seuss captures the magic of love, where reality becomes more beautiful than the dreams we once chased. It highlights the power of love to transform our lives.

Overview of the Person:

Dr. Seuss, born Theodor Seuss Geisel, was an American children's author, illustrator, and cartoonist, famous for his imaginative stories and playful rhymes.

53-"You only live once, but if you do it right, once is enough."

— Mae West

Comment:

Mae West's quote underscores the importance of living life to the fullest. It serves as a reminder to make the most of our time by pursuing meaningful and fulfilling experiences.

Overview of the Person:

Mae West was an American actress, singer, playwright, and comedian, known for her wit, humor, and influence on the entertainment industry in the early 20th century.

54-"If you want to know what a man's like, take a good look at how he treats his inferiors, not his equals."

— J.K. Rowling, *Harry Potter and the Goblet of Fire*

Comment:

Rowling's quote emphasizes the significance of empathy and character. It suggests that true morality is revealed in how we treat those with less power or status.

Overview of the Person:

J.K. Rowling is a British author best known for creating the *Harry Potter* series, which has become one of the best-selling book series in history and inspired a global phenomenon.

55-*"Don't walk in front of me... I may not follow*
Don't walk behind me... I may not lead
Walk beside me... just be my friend."

— *Albert Camus*

Comment:

Camus' quote reflects the essence of true friendship, where equality, companionship, and mutual support are valued. It encourages us to seek relationships that are built on partnership rather than hierarchy.

Overview of the Person:

Albert Camus was a French philosopher, author, and journalist, known for his contributions to existentialism and absurdism, as well as for his works like *The Stranger* and *The Myth of Sisyphus*.

56-"I've learned that people will forget what you said, people will forget what you did, but people will never forget how you made them feel."

— *Maya Angelou*

Comment:

Angelou's quote emphasizes the lasting impact of emotions. It reminds us that the way we treat others can leave a deep and enduring impression, far beyond words or actions.

Overview of the Person:

Maya Angelou was a renowned American poet, memoirist, and civil rights activist who used her writing and public speaking to inspire social change and promote equality.

57-"It is better to be hated for what you are than to be loved for what you are not."

— Andre Gide, Autumn Leaves

Comment:

Gide's quote emphasizes the value of authenticity. It encourages embracing one's true self, even at the risk of rejection, rather than conforming to win the approval of others.

Overview of the Person:

Andre Gide was a French author and Nobel Prize laureate in literature, known for his exploration of morality, self-discovery, and individual freedom in his works.

58-"Twenty years from now you will be more disappointed by the things that you didn't do than by the ones you did do. So throw off the bowlines. Sail away from the safe harbor. Catch the trade winds in your sails. Explore. Dream. Discover."

— H. Jackson Brown Jr., P.S. I Love You

Comment:

Brown's quote encourages us to take risks and seek adventure. It serves as a reminder that regrets often come from missed opportunities rather than failed attempts.

Overview of the Person:

H. Jackson Brown Jr. is an American author best known for his inspirational book *Life's Little Instruction Book*, which offers practical advice for living a fulfilling life.

59-"Imperfection is beauty, madness is genius and it's better to be absolutely ridiculous than absolutely boring."

— Marilyn Monroe

Comment:

Monroe's quote celebrates the uniqueness found in flaws and eccentricities. It reminds us that embracing our imperfections can be more fulfilling than striving for an unrealistic ideal.

Overview of the Person:

Marilyn Monroe was an iconic American actress and cultural symbol of the 20th century, known for her beauty, acting talent, and thought-provoking insights.

60-*"Good friends, good books, and a sleepy conscience: this is the ideal life."*

— Mark Twain

Comment:

Twain's quote captures the essence of a simple and fulfilling life. It highlights the importance of companionship, knowledge, and peace of mind.

Overview of the Person:

Mark Twain, born Samuel Langhorne Clemens, was an American author and humorist, famous for works such as *The Adventures of Tom Sawyer* and *Adventures of Huckleberry Finn*.

61-"The fool doth think he is wise, but the wise man knows himself to be a fool."

— *William Shakespeare*

Comment:

Shakespeare's quote speaks to the nature of wisdom and self-awareness. It suggests that true wisdom involves recognizing the limits of one's own knowledge.

Overview of the Person:

William Shakespeare was an English playwright and poet, widely regarded as one of the greatest writers in the English language and known for works like *Hamlet*, *Macbeth*, and *Romeo and Juliet*.

62-*"Yesterday is history, tomorrow is a mystery, today is a gift of God, which is why we call it the present."*

— *Bill Keane*

Comment:

Keane's quote reminds us to appreciate the present moment. It encourages us to focus on the here and now, rather than dwelling on the past or worrying about the future.

Overview of the Person:

Bill Keane was an American cartoonist, best known for his popular comic strip *The Family Circus*, which humorously portrayed family life.

63-"I have not failed. I've just found 10,000 ways that won't work."

— *Thomas A. Edison*

Comment:

Edison's quote reflects a resilient mindset toward failure, viewing it as a step toward success rather than a setback. It serves as a reminder to persist in the face of challenges.

Overview of the Person:

Thomas A. Edison was an American inventor and businessman, known for developing many devices, including the phonograph and the practical electric light bulb.

64-*"It is not a lack of love, but a lack of friendship that makes unhappy marriages."*

— *Friedrich Nietzsche*

Comment:

Nietzsche's quote emphasizes the importance of companionship and mutual understanding in a successful relationship, suggesting that friendship is the foundation of lasting love.

Overview of the Person:

Friedrich Nietzsche was a German philosopher and cultural critic, known for his works on existentialism, nihilism, and the nature of human existence.

65-"The opposite of love is not hate, it's indifference. The opposite of art is not ugliness, it's indifference. The opposite of faith is not heresy, it's indifference. And the opposite of life is not death, it's indifference."

— Elie Wiesel

Comment:

Wiesel's quote underscores the destructive power of indifference. It reminds us that apathy can cause more harm than active opposition because it shows a lack of care or concern.

Overview of the Person:
Elie Wiesel was a Romanian-born American writer, professor, and Holocaust survivor who authored several works on his experiences during the Holocaust, including *Night*.

66-*"The man who does not read has no advantage over the man who cannot read."*

— *Mark Twain*

Comment:

Twain's quote highlights the value of lifelong learning and the transformative power of reading. It suggests that the ability to read is meaningless without the willingness to use it.

Overview of the Person:

Mark Twain, born Samuel Langhorne Clemens, was an American author and humorist, celebrated for his wit and works such as *The Adventures of Tom Sawyer*.

67-"A reader lives a thousand lives before he dies, said Jojen. The man who never reads lives only one."

— *George R.R. Martin, A Dance with Dragons*

Comment:

Martin's quote captures the magic of reading, which allows us to experience countless adventures and perspectives. It emphasizes the richness that stories bring to life.

Overview of the Person:

George R.R. Martin is an American novelist and short story writer, best known for his *A Song of Ice and Fire* series, which inspired the television show *Game of Thrones*.

68-"For every minute you are angry you lose sixty seconds of happiness."

— *Ralph Waldo Emerson*

Comment:

Emerson's quote encourages us to let go of anger and embrace positive emotions. It serves as a reminder to cherish moments of happiness rather than wasting them on negative feelings.

Overview of the Person:

Ralph Waldo Emerson was an American essayist, philosopher, and poet, a central figure in the Transcendentalist movement, who advocated for individualism and nature.

69-*"I'm not upset that you lied to me, I'm upset that from now on I can't believe you."*

— *Friedrich Nietzsche*

Comment:

Nietzsche's quote reflects on the lasting damage caused by dishonesty. It underscores the importance of trust in relationships and the difficulty in restoring it once broken.

Overview of the Person:

Friedrich Nietzsche was a German philosopher whose works have had a profound impact on Western thought, including themes of morality, religion, and existentialism.

70-*"If you can't explain it to a six-year-old, you don't understand it yourself."*

— *Albert Einstein*

Comment:

Einstein's quote emphasizes the importance of clarity and simplicity in understanding complex concepts. It suggests that true mastery involves the ability to communicate ideas in a straightforward way.

Overview of the Person:

Albert Einstein was a theoretical physicist whose groundbreaking theories on relativity reshaped our understanding of space, time, and energy.

71-"Love is that condition in which the happiness of another person is essential to your own."

— _Robert A. Heinlein, Stranger in a Strange Land_

Comment:

Heinlein's quote captures the selfless nature of true love, where another person's joy becomes integral to one's own well-being. It reflects a deep connection that goes beyond individual desires.

Overview of the Person:

Robert A. Heinlein was an American science fiction writer, known for his influential works such as _Stranger in a Strange Land_ and _Starship Troopers_, which often explored social and philosophical themes.

72-"I have always imagined that Paradise will be a kind of library."

— Jorge Luis Borges

Comment:

Borges' quote expresses a love for literature and the knowledge that books provide. It suggests that an ideal world is one where learning and imagination thrive.

Overview of the Person:

Jorge Luis Borges was an Argentine writer, poet, and essayist, renowned for his imaginative and often philosophical short stories that explore concepts of time, identity, and reality.

73-*"Life isn't about finding yourself. Life is about creating yourself."*

— *George Bernard Shaw*

Comment:

Shaw's quote challenges the idea of passive self-discovery, advocating instead for active self-creation. It encourages individuals to shape their own identity through choices and actions.

Overview of the Person:

George Bernard Shaw was an Irish playwright, critic, and polemicist whose works, including *Pygmalion*, often addressed social issues with humor and wit.

74-"If you want your children to be intelligent, read them fairy tales. If you want them to be more intelligent, read them more fairy tales."

— *Albert Einstein*

Comment:

Einstein's quote highlights the value of imagination in intellectual development. It suggests that creativity and storytelling play a vital role in fostering a child's cognitive growth.

Overview of the Person:

Albert Einstein was a theoretical physicist whose theories of relativity significantly influenced modern physics. He was also an advocate for education and creativity.

75-"The truth is, everyone is going to hurt you. You just got to find the ones worth suffering for."

— Bob Marley

Comment:

Marley's quote reflects the inevitability of pain in relationships but also acknowledges the value of enduring challenges for the sake of meaningful connections.

Overview of the Person:

Bob Marley was a Jamaican singer, songwriter, and cultural icon, known for popularizing reggae music and promoting messages of peace, love, and social justice.

76-"Do what you can, with what you have, where you are."

— *Theodore Roosevelt*

Comment:

Roosevelt's quote encourages making the best of any situation by taking action, regardless of circumstances. It serves as a call for resourcefulness and determination.

Overview of the Person:

Theodore Roosevelt was the 26th President of the United States, known for his progressive policies, conservation efforts, and the establishment of the national park system.

77-"Love is like the wind, you can't see it but you can feel it."

— Nicholas Sparks, A Walk to Remember

Comment:

Sparks' quote poetically describes love as an intangible yet powerful force. It suggests that while love may not always be visible, its presence is deeply felt.

Overview of the Person:

Nicholas Sparks is an American novelist and screenwriter known for his romantic fiction, including *The Notebook* and *A Walk to Remember*, which have been adapted into popular films.

78-"Common sense is not so common."

— Voltaire

Comment:

Voltaire's quote challenges the idea that common sense is universally shared. It implies that practical judgment is surprisingly rare, even though it is often taken for granted.

Overview of the Person:

Voltaire was a French Enlightenment writer, philosopher, and historian, known for his wit, criticism of the Church, and advocacy for civil liberties and freedom of expression.

79-"Be alone, that is when ideas are born."

— *Nikola Tesla*

Comment:

Tesla's quote suggests that solitude is essential for creativity and innovation. It highlights the value of introspection and personal time for generating new ideas.

Overview of the Person:

Nikola Tesla was a Serbian-American inventor and engineer, best known for his contributions to the development of alternating current (AC) electricity, radio technology, and numerous other innovations.

80-"Before you embark on a journey of revenge, dig two graves."

— Confucius

Comment:

Confucius' quote serves as a cautionary reminder about the destructive consequences of seeking revenge, suggesting that it often harms both the victim and the avenger.

Overview of the Person:

Confucius was a Chinese philosopher and teacher whose teachings, focusing on morality, family loyalty, and social harmony, deeply influenced Chinese culture and philosophy.

81-"Dead people receive more flowers than the living ones because regret is stronger than gratitude."

— *Anne Frank*

Comment:

Anne Frank's quote reflects on human tendencies to express appreciation too late, highlighting the power of regret compared to the often-overlooked act of gratitude.

Overview of the Person:

Anne Frank was a Jewish girl who wrote a diary while hiding during the Holocaust. Her writings provide a poignant perspective on the experiences of Jews during World War II.

82-*"If you want the present to be different from the past, study the past."*

— *Baruch Spinoza*

Comment:

Spinoza's quote underscores the importance of learning from history to avoid repeating mistakes. It suggests that understanding past events is key to making meaningful changes in the present.

Overview of the Person:

Baruch Spinoza was a Dutch philosopher of Sephardi Jewish origin, known for his work in ethics and rationalism. His ideas helped lay the groundwork for the Enlightenment.

83-"Above all, don't lie to yourself."

— *Fyodor Dostoevsky*

Comment:

Dostoevsky's quote emphasizes the importance of self-honesty. It suggests that personal growth and integrity begin with the courage to confront one's own truths.

Overview of the Person:

Fyodor Dostoevsky was a Russian novelist and philosopher, known for works such as *Crime and Punishment* and *The Brothers Karamazov*, which explore complex psychological and moral themes.

84-"Your knowledge is far more important than your degree."

— Paul Dirac

Comment:

Dirac's quote challenges the conventional emphasis on formal education, highlighting the true value of practical knowledge and understanding over mere credentials.

Overview of the Person:

Paul Dirac was a British theoretical physicist and a founder of quantum mechanics. His work in quantum theory and contributions to the field earned him the Nobel Prize in Physics.

85-*"Trust in God, but tie your camel."*

— Arab proverb

Comment:

This proverb encourages a balance between faith and practicality. It suggests that while one should trust in divine will, it is also important to take responsible actions to ensure one's safety.

Overview of the Saying:

This saying reflects a practical approach to life commonly found in Islamic teachings, emphasizing the importance of both reliance on God and personal effort.

86-"Seek knowledge from the cradle to the grave."

— Imam Ali

Comment:

This saying stresses the lifelong pursuit of knowledge. It encourages continuous learning and growth as a means to better oneself and society.

Overview of the Person:

Imam Ali was the cousin and son-in-law of Prophet Muhammad (PBUH) and the fourth caliph in Islamic history. He is highly regarded for his wisdom, piety, and contributions to Islamic thought.

87-"The only true wisdom is in knowing you know nothing."

— *Socrates*

Comment:

This quote emphasizes the importance of humility in the pursuit of knowledge. It suggests that acknowledging one's ignorance is the first step toward gaining true understanding.

Overview of the Person:

Socrates was an ancient Greek philosopher who is credited with laying the foundation of Western philosophy. His teachings often focused on ethics, self-knowledge, and the Socratic method of inquiry.

88-"Life is really simple, but we insist on making it complicated."

— Confucius

Comment:

Confucius highlights the tendency of human beings to overcomplicate life. The message encourages simplifying one's approach to find peace and contentment.

Overview of the Person:

Confucius was a Chinese philosopher and teacher whose teachings on morality, government, and social relationships have profoundly influenced Chinese culture and other East Asian societies.

89-"Do not go where the path may lead, go instead where there is no path and leave a trail."

— *Ralph Waldo Emerson*

Comment:

This quote inspires individuality and the courage to forge one's own way in life rather than conforming to established norms.

Overview of the Person:

Ralph Waldo Emerson was an American philosopher, essayist, and poet who championed the idea of transcendentalism, advocating for self-reliance, intuition, and the inherent goodness of people.

90-"The only thing necessary for the triumph of evil is for good men to do nothing."

— *Edmund Burke*

Comment:

Burke's quote stresses the responsibility of individuals to act against injustice, warning that inaction allows evil to prevail.

Overview of the Person:

Edmund Burke was an Irish statesman, philosopher, and political theorist known for his support of the American Revolution and criticism of the French Revolution.

91-"Man suffers only because he takes seriously what the gods made for fun."

— Alan Watts

Comment:

Watts humorously suggests that life is meant to be enjoyed and that taking it too seriously causes unnecessary suffering.

Overview of the Person:

Alan Watts was a British philosopher who popularized Eastern philosophy for a Western audience, focusing on Zen Buddhism, Taoism, and other spiritual traditions.

92-"Patience is bitter, but its fruit is sweet."

— Aristotle

Comment:

Aristotle's quote reflects the idea that enduring difficulties is often challenging, but the rewards for persevering are worth the struggle.

Overview of the Person:

Aristotle was an ancient Greek philosopher and scientist who made significant contributions to various fields, including ethics, politics, metaphysics, and natural sciences.

93-*"Silence is a source of great strength."*

— *Lao Tzu*

Comment:

This quote emphasizes the power of quiet contemplation and the strength that can be found in stillness and introspection.

Overview of the Person:

Lao Tzu is a central figure in Chinese culture and is traditionally considered the author of the "Tao Te Ching" and the founder of Taoism, which emphasizes living in harmony with the Tao, or "the way."

94-"It always seems impossible until it's done."

— Nelson Mandela

Comment:

Mandela's quote inspires perseverance by reminding us that even the most challenging tasks appear unachievable until they are accomplished.

Overview of the Person:

Nelson Mandela was a South African anti-apartheid revolutionary and political leader who served as President of South Africa. He was a symbol of the struggle for freedom and equality.

95-"In a time of deceit, telling the truth is a revolutionary act."

— *George Orwell*

Comment:

Orwell's quote underscores the courage required to be honest in a society where dishonesty is the norm, framing truth-telling as a form of resistance.

Overview of the Person:

George Orwell was an English novelist, essayist, and critic, best known for his dystopian novels *1984* and *Animal Farm*, which explore themes of totalitarianism and political manipulation.

96-"I would rather die of passion than of boredom."

— Vincent van Gogh

Comment:

Van Gogh's quote expresses a preference for a life driven by intense emotions and creativity over one of complacency and monotony.

Overview of the Person:

Vincent van Gogh was a Dutch post-impressionist painter whose works are celebrated for their emotional depth, bold color, and distinct style, despite his struggles with mental health.

97-"Knowledge speaks, but wisdom listens."

— *Jimi Hendrix*

Comment:

Hendrix's quote highlights the distinction between simply possessing information and having the wisdom to be attentive and learn from others, emphasizing the power of listening.

Overview of the Person:

Jimi Hendrix was an iconic American rock guitarist, singer, and songwriter, known for his innovative electric guitar techniques and his influence on the development of modern music.

98-"I would rather be a little nobody, than to be an evil somebody."

— Abraham Lincoln

Comment:

Lincoln's quote reflects the value of integrity and humility, suggesting that it is better to live a simple, ethical life than to gain fame through harmful actions.

Overview of the Person:

Abraham Lincoln was the 16th President of the United States, known for leading the country during the Civil War and for his efforts to abolish slavery.

99-*"The man who asks a question is a fool for a minute, the man who does not ask is a fool for life."*

— Confucius

Comment:

Confucius highlights the value of curiosity and learning, stressing that asking questions is a crucial step toward gaining wisdom, even if it initially exposes ignorance.

Overview of the Person:

Confucius was an ancient Chinese philosopher and teacher whose teachings formed the basis of Confucianism, focusing on morality, social relationships, and justice.

100-"The best among you are those who have the best manners and character."

– Prophet Muhammad, peace be upon him

Comment:

This saying highlights the importance of good conduct and ethics in Islam, emphasizing that true excellence is measured by one's behavior and treatment of others.

Overview of the Person:

The Prophet Muhammad's teachings often emphasized the significance of character, kindness, and ethical behavior as core values in a Muslim's life.

Final Thoughts

As we come to the end of this collection of quotes, I hope you've found
inspiration and wisdom that resonates with you. Quotes have a unique
power to encapsulate profound thoughts in just a few words, offering
us new perspectives and encouraging us to reflect on our lives.
Whether you read them in moments of joy or times of challenge, may
these sayings serve as a reminder of the beauty and complexity of the
human experience. Carry them with you, share them, and let them
inspire your journey.

Acknowledgments

I would like to express my heartfelt gratitude to all those who
supported me during the creation of this book. To my family and
friends, your encouragement and belief in my vision made this
possible. To the thinkers and writers whose words have inspired
countless individuals, including myself, thank you for sharing your
insights with the world. Lastly, to you, the reader—thank you for

taking the time to engage with these quotes. May they bring you light and motivation in your everyday life.

Author's Note

Writing this book has been a journey filled with reflection and discovery. I've always believed in the power of words to uplift and inspire, and compiling these quotes has deepened my appreciation for the wisdom shared by so many remarkable individuals throughout history. One quote that particularly resonates with me is, *"Life isn't about finding yourself. Life is about creating yourself."* – George Bernard Shaw. It reminds me that we are the authors of our own stories, capable of shaping our destinies through our choices and actions.

My Gmail account to receive any suggestions :
mogad2communicate@gmail.com

"The future belongs to those who believe in the beauty of their dreams."

– Eleanor Roosevelt